My Street

Written by Shelley Jones
Illustrated by Chantal Stewart

I live on a little street.
On my street, there are
many different houses.

2

3

We live at number 12.
Our house is a brick house.
It is a single-story house
and our yard is in the back.

4

I like to sit on the front porch
and talk with Mrs. Price next door.
She lives alone.
Her children are all grown-up now,
and they live far away.

5

6

The big brick house next door to
Mrs. Price was sold last month.

The new family moved in yesterday.
The moving van was full of furniture
and boxes.
There were toys in the boxes.

James and Samantha live
at number 17 with their
dog, Max. Sometimes
I play with Max.

There is a big stack of bricks
in the front yard because workers are
building a new fireplace and chimney.

There is a big motorcycle
parked in front of number 21.
It belongs to Jim.
Jim likes loud music.
He plays in a band.

I like to watch Jim
ride his motorcycle.
He waves to me as he rides
down our street.

From my porch, I can see the
birds on the roof of number 23.
George and his brother Ron
feed the birds.

Sometimes I help George feed
them. The brown and white
bird is very tame. It takes bread
from my hand.

13

Jane lives in the two-story brick house at the end of the street. Her house has a flower bed in front.

Jane likes to play her violin. She has a music stand in her front room. When I walk past her house, I can hear her playing.

14

15

I like living on my street.
There is so much to see and do.